THE GREATEST MAGICIAN
THAT EVER CAME TO BE

Vera Adjin

THE
GREATEST MAGICIAN
THAT EVER CAME TO BE

Vera Adjin

THE GREATEST MAGICIAN
THAT EVER CAME TO BE

Vera Adjin

Books Academy LLC
112 SW H K Dodgen Loop
Temple, Texas 76504
Hotline: (254) 800-1189

Ordering Information:
Quantity sales. Special discounts are available on quantity purchases by corporations, associations, and others. For details, contact the publisher at the address above.

Printed in the United States of America.

ISBN-13:   Paperback   978-1-966567-16-5
             eBook   978-1-966567-17-2

Library of Congress Control Number: 2025901217

ACKNOWLEDGEMENT

I just want to thank Mr. Hebert and the entire Mindstir Media, including my editor, Mr. Rob Rop, and my illustrator, Mr. Justin Stier, for the great work they did with my script I also want to thank my life partner, Kwame Adjin, and my children: Anastasia, James, Emmanuel, Richard, Christopher, and Veronica for their endless love and encouragements. I extend my deepest gratitude to the following families and individuals: The Wreh family, the Kwofie family, the Ansanyi family, the Ackom family, the Pobee family, the Revived Church of God family, the Yankson family, and Theresa Bacani. I also want to send lots of love to my grandchildren: Ernest, EJ, Elianna Mary, Eliora Vera and Serene Paris. I send love to my in-laws, my nursing school study partners during my Seton Hall University years, professor Veronica at Hostos Community College, my god mother Mina Ankrah, and my god children Nathaniel Asare, Eva Princess Acheampong, and Joy Fuentes, I also want to express gratitude to all my co-workers at Bronx Lebanon Special Care Center, Concourse rehab and nursing center, Maxim Home Care, T.F.C. Service Bureau, White Glove Community Care, and Promise Care Agency. Last but not the least, to my childhood friends: Cecilia Koomson, Victoria Yankson, and Grace Wood, thank you for your support. Thank you to Pastors and pastoral related personnel, all the various Law Enforcement Agencies, all Veterans, all Heath care Workers, Teachers, Journalists, Actors, Actresses, TKD ladies club members, and the entire Ghanaian Community for

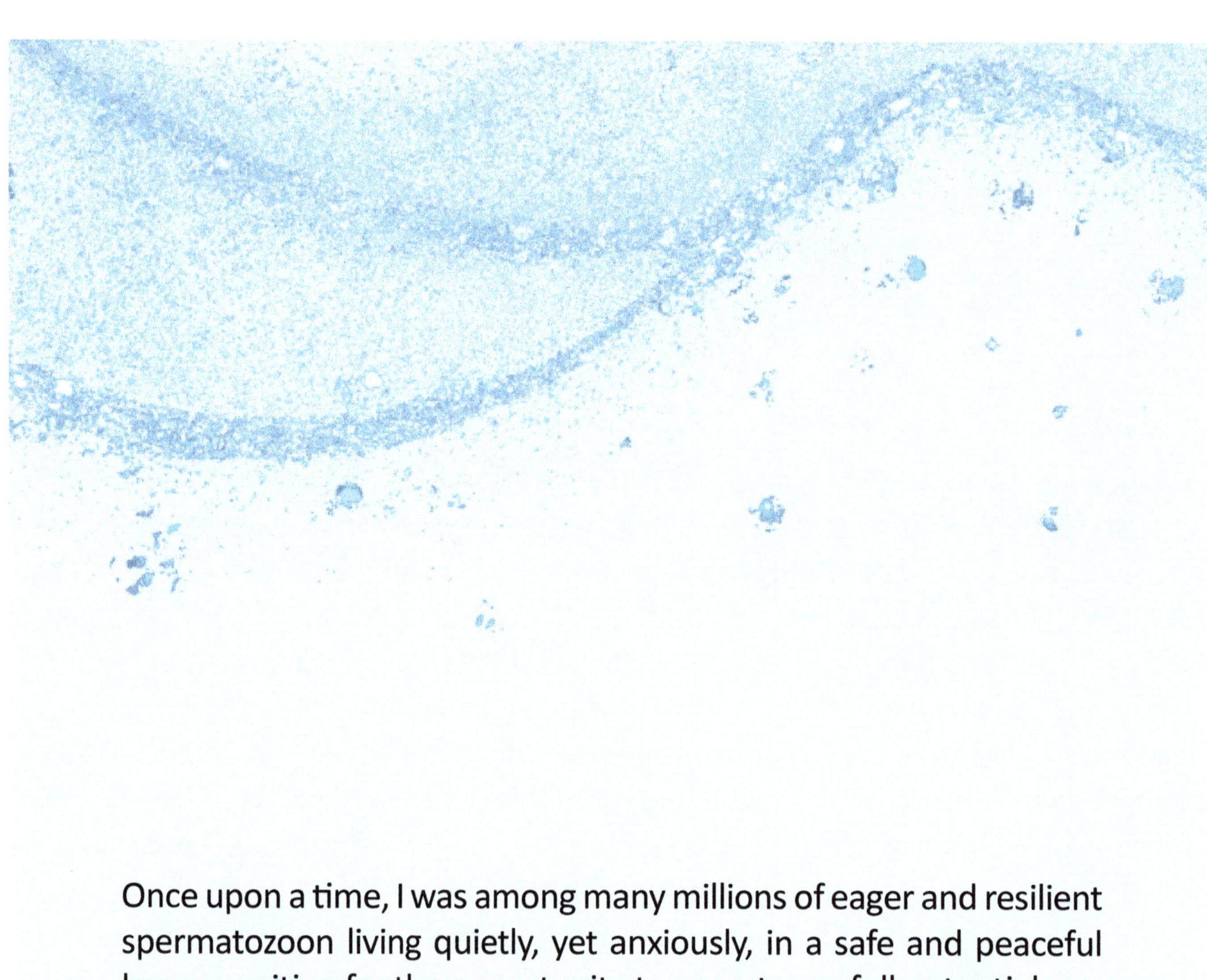

Once upon a time, I was among many millions of eager and resilient spermatozoon living quietly, yet anxiously, in a safe and peaceful haven, waiting for the opportunity to grow to my full potential.

One day I found myself swimming with many great champions to an unknown territory. With lots of luck and hard work, I found myself alone in a hollow tube at a place called Ovary Land. For four days and four nights I wondered about what to do to survive at Ovary Land, and how to get to my final destination.

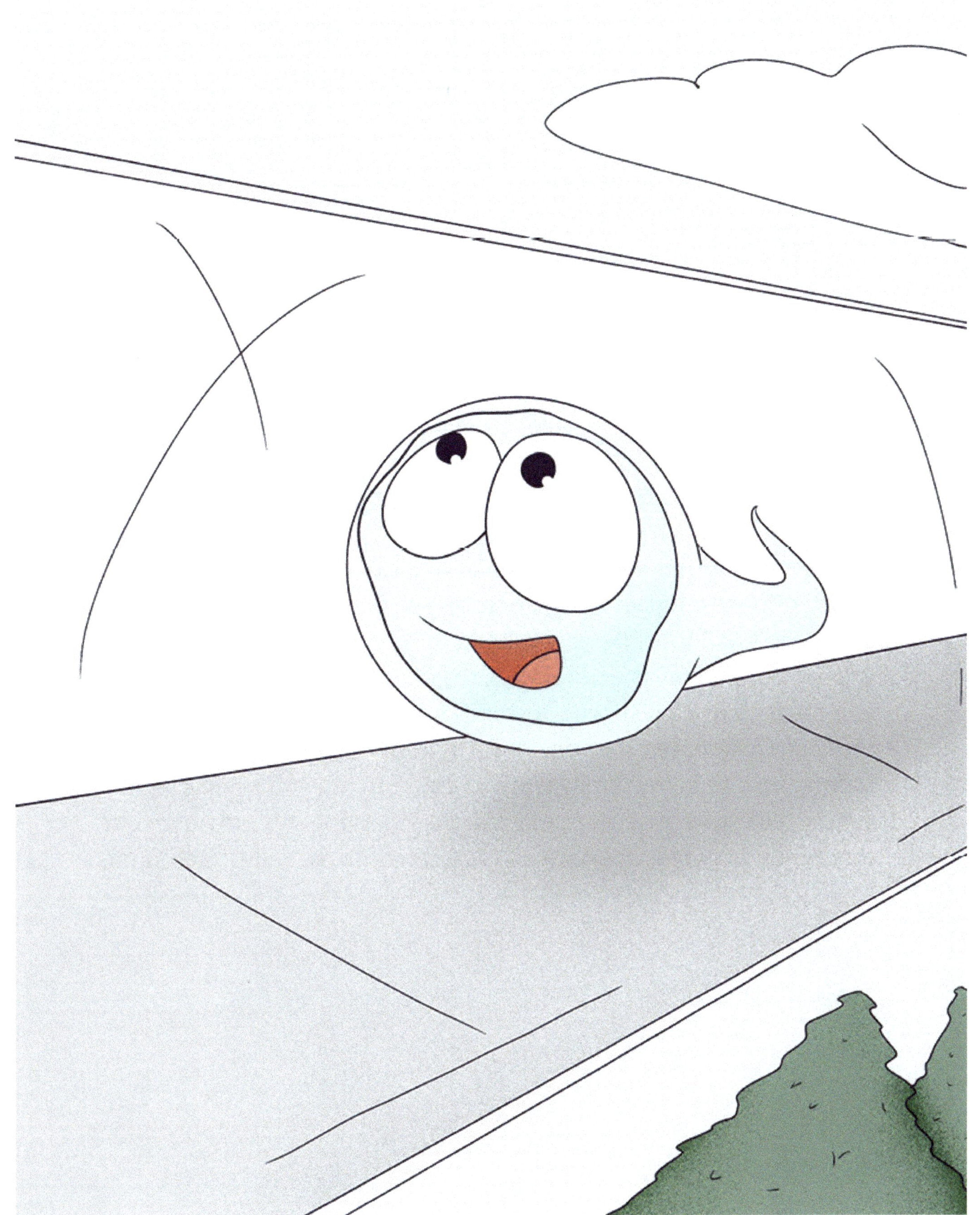

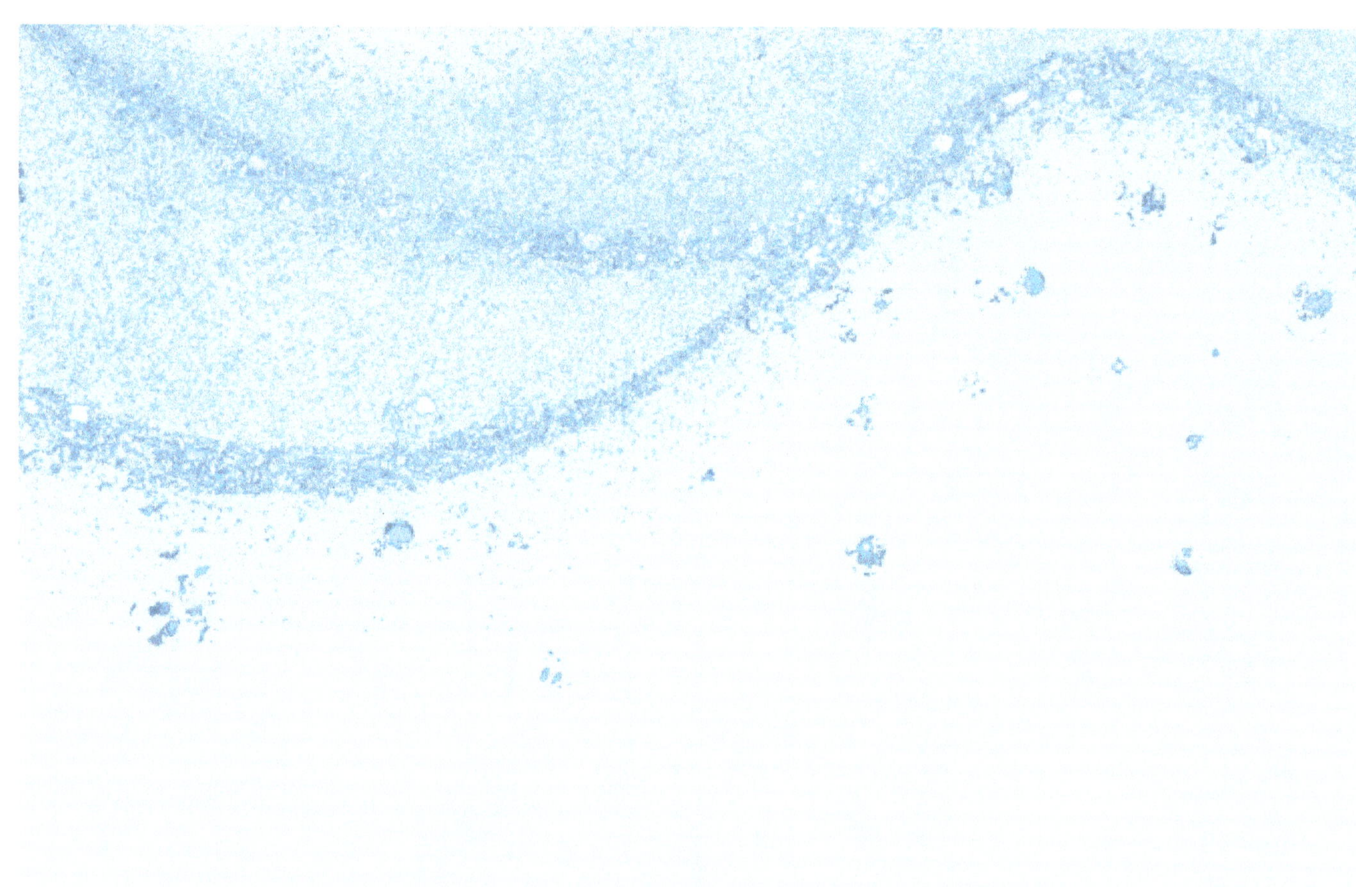

Then I remembered what my ancestors always talked about around the camp fire about the enchanted and beautiful Wish Castle. This is what they said all the time. First, to get to the magical Wish Castle you must be a great sticky substance swimmer and must definitely meet an Oocyte. Yes, an Oocyte which nobody has ever seen or met before; no one in my family knows what and how an Oocyte is, but yet my ancestors are sure, and insist that meeting this unknown but renowned Oocyte is the only way I can grow to my fullest potential.

On the fifth day, as I was wiggling back and forth and wondering about what being at my fullest potential would look like, I finally met Oocyte at a place called Fallopian Street, a little way from Uterus City and close to Ovary Land.

"Oocyte, Oh my God! My ancestors talked about you all the time, I never thought I would ever meet you."

With a quivering, sweet voice she responded, "Yes, I am Oocyte. Yes, I am real and I exist only under a weird circumstance.

"My ancestors are the only ones that live in this domain and hold the key to the secret castle. We are travelers, and we never return home once we leave. Before I left home, my parents told me my survival depends on me being kind to a wiggler, also known as a spermicide. They are the only strange things that wander around in our land."

Oocyte told me the secret code to magical Wish Castle, which includes a great, big hug and a fantasy walk up to ten days across a sticky wet land After a lengthy conversation, we came to a conclusion that none of us can survive this journey without the other's help. So, we sealed our conversation with a lovely hug, where the two become one, resulting in a Zygote.

I continued my fantasy walk for up to ten days. During my walk, everything I needed I received, which made me feel enriched, emboldened and empowered.

"Hello, I'm Zygote and I contain 23 chromosomes of my father and 23 chromosomes of my mother; that makes me very, very special."

I continued my journey to Wish Castle with my secret wish list, wanting to grow to my full potential. After several days, I arrived at Wish Castle, the most beautiful, multicolored, magical place I have ever imagined.

Oh no, what if my wish does not come true, or what if I waste my wish on unnecessary things. For once I felt scared, confused and alone. What am I going to do? And then I heard a voice say, "Calm down, Zygote, for I will always be with you till you reach your fullest potential." Immediately, I felt a sense of relief, calm, and excitement again.

I have only four wishes and so I have to think carefully and plan wisely before I make any wish. Hmm, as I paced back and forth, what will be my best first wish? I thought cautiously. I remember Oocyte told me that my first three wishes will take ninety days each to come full circle, that means I will be here a while. Yes! Yes! Yes! I know how I am going to do this, I am so excited and intrigued at the same time.

Hello! Hello, Wish Castle, my name is Zygote and I wish to grow my first trimester's figures healthily while I relax comfortably in the castle. Immediately, I felt energized, exuberant and protected, as if I were in a sweet, scented, unbreakable bobble. I sighed with relief; this feels good, I could get used to this. I am so happy and ready for whatever is to come next.

From that moment onwards, I began to change, slowly but consistently. Every day something different is happening to me; this is so very exciting. A neural tube along my back is closing, a brain and spinal cord are developing from the neural tube. A heart and lungs are starting to form. The structures for eyes and ears are also developing. A stomach is forming. Everything is coming together perfectly.

Hallelujah! Hallelujah, I am blessed. I feel active and fabulous. What a wonderful feeling.

So it came to pass after ninety days I made my second wish. Wish Castle, Wish Castle, for my second wish, I wish to grow all my second trimester's figures healthily while I relax comfortably in the castle.

After another ninety days my entire body began to show more and more of what I have surprisingly anticipated, and it was excellent. I began waving my body from side to side and humming: hmm hmm hmm hmm hmm hmm hmm. I feel so good, no amount of words can describe how I'm feeling. And every day I keep on moving back and forth, stretching, jumping and humming a sweet melody in my mind.

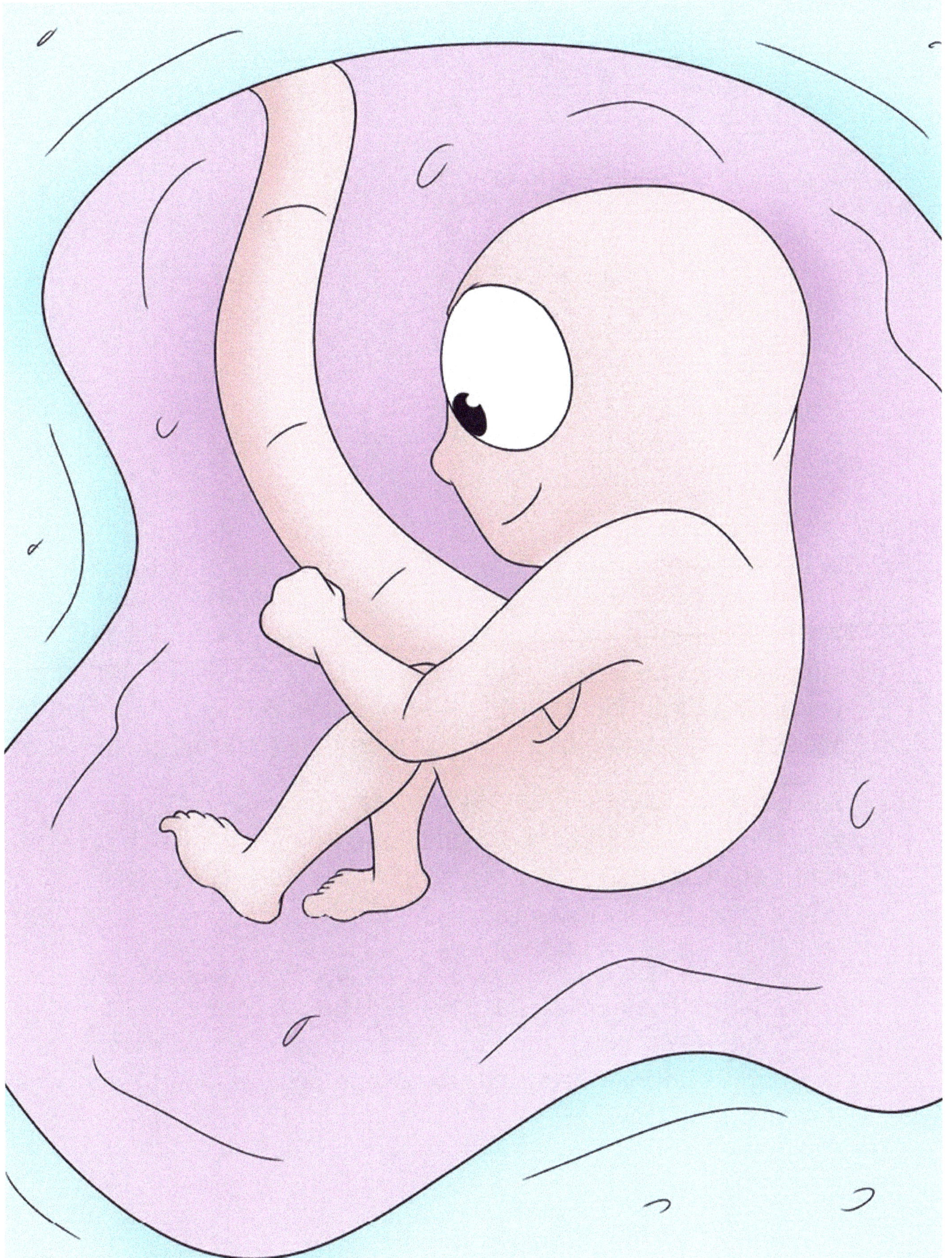

My bones grow stronger, I see fingers, toes, and nails that are well shaped. I feel eyebrows, eyelids and eyelashes uniquely in place with tiny, fine hair all over my body. I have beautiful, dark, curly hair on my head. I look and feel sensational; this is better than I expected. I began jumping up and down more and more and swimming faster than before. I began kicking hard more and more, and it felt great.

I feel like I have everything figured out. Wow! Life is good. I cannot wait for my next surprise. Hey Wish Castle, Wish Castle, I wish to grow my third trimester's figures healthily while I relax comfortably in the castle.

And so, for the next ninety days my lungs fully develop and I can breathe better. I have reflexes that are well coordinated I can blink, open and close my eyes. I can turn my head from side to side and grasp firmly with my fingers. And I can also respond to sound, light and touch instantaneously.

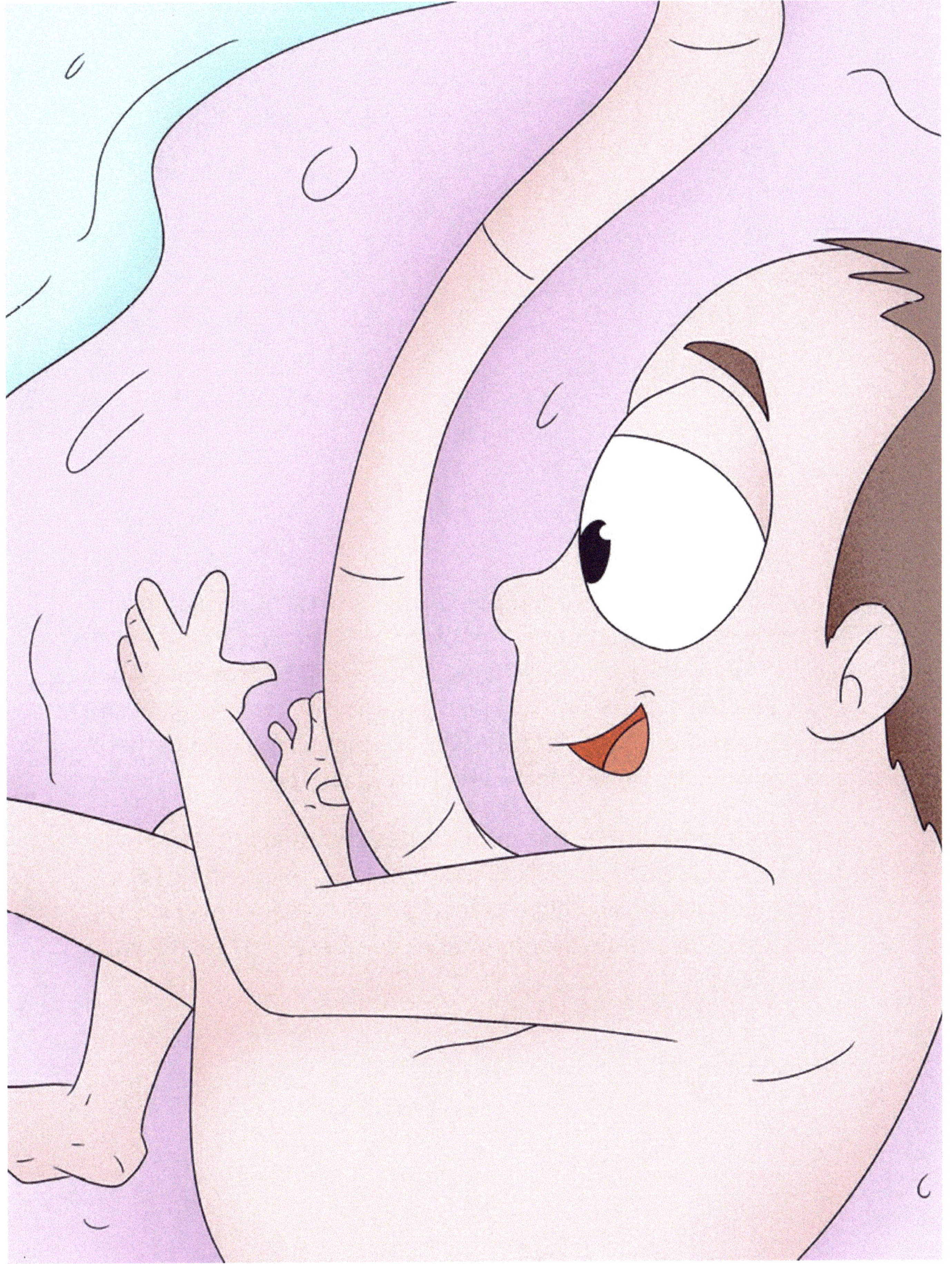

I have finally reached my potential. Oh my God! I am fully grown, am fully grown. Thank you, Lord. I kept running, dancing, jumping and making funny noises in Wish Castle. That was the most incredible and memorable day of my life. I feel matured, so matured, and I am ready to move out of Wish Castle, Oh, I cannot wait to go out there and see what the outside looks like, I am so excited.

In the morning, I cleaned the entire castle neatly and put everything in place, and I said to myself even though I can get anything I want in here and I can do anything I want, I think it's about time to leave Wish Castle, for there is a lot to explore out there and I cannot wait to get there.

So in the evening, I started looking for a way out of Wish Castle. For hours and hours I kept on looking, but the entire Wish Castle was sealed shut. Oh no, how am I going to get out of here? I began to cry, and as soon as I started crying I heard the same voice that calmed me down before when I was scared saying, "Do not worry, you've got this, use your last wish." Because of my over excitement I had totally forgotten my last wish, which I was told by Oocyte will only take a few minutes to a few hours to come true.

I immediately stopped crying and calmed myself down. I began to sing my good-bye song to Wish Castle, for in the heat of the excitement I forgot to tell Wish Castle how I appreciate all the things I have gotten during my stay. The energy, the good time, care and kindness which will never be forgotten, and most of all the breath of life. Thank you so very, very, much Wish Castle. You are and will always be my greatest hero.

Now that I have properly said good-bye, I am ready to leave Wish Castle. Wish Castle, please open your hidden door and fly me gently and safely to the real world.

As soon as I said this, an amazing, small, wooden gate opened. I quickly swam through and before the gate could close, a second shimmering crystal, medium-sized gate opened in front of me. Oh my, I am being treated like royalty and it feels marvelous.

Good bye
and
be safe

By the time I passed through the second gate, there comes yet another large shiny, golden gate, with rainbow stripes across from side to side and the words Good-bye and Be Safe written in bright red in the middle of the gate. I think it was Wish Castle wishing me God Speed.

I gave the sign a thumbs up, blinked twice, and landed in the most gentle and soft hands of my giant Mommy, with my giant Daddy nearby.

The end.

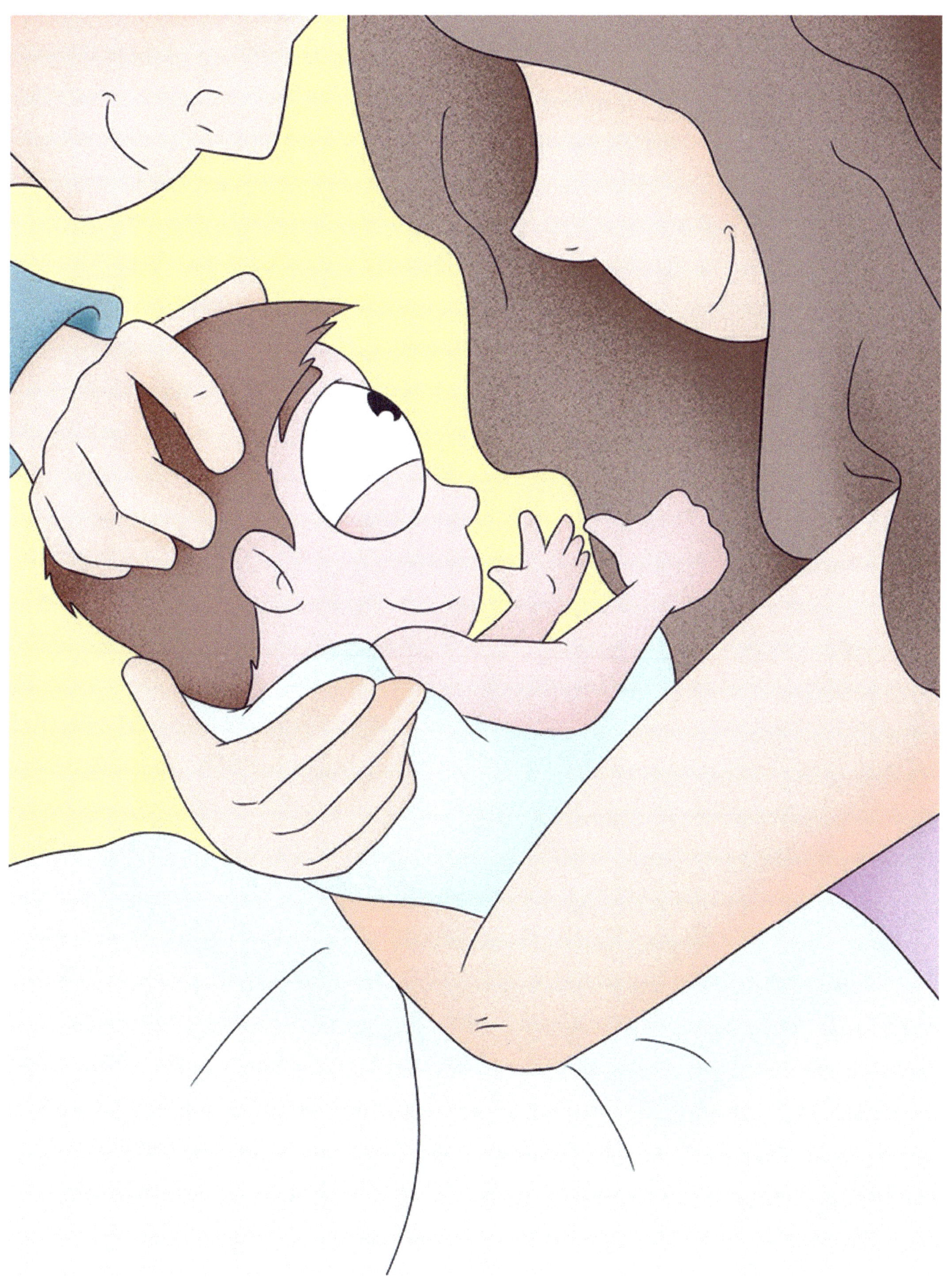

Welcome to your fruit experience. You will see that there are fruits that are more recognizable than others, we challenge you to guess which fruit you will paint at all times.

A word of advice: paint as you like, at any time.

This Book Belong to: